The New Guide to Master Money Mindset and Wealth 2021

Contents

Introduction

A large number of us understand what we should do with regards to fundamental money management – spend short of what you procure, spare a secret stash, and invest for retirement. Notwithstanding, setting up great propensities is consistently more difficult than one might expect.

Money management, in the same way as other significant things throughout everyday life, requires discipline. Also, discipline is certainly not a characteristic mental state for consistency. Add to that the blame and disgrace that a few of us convey with regards to finances, and you have a formula for money management wretchedness. Or then again, in any event, a feeling of why the "ostrich approach" can appear to be more engaging than handling fundamental issues.

In any case, as engaging as it might appear, there is not a solitary financial master pushing the ostrich approach as a way to accomplishing financial wellness! Indeed, going that course will just present more blame and disgrace over the long haul.

Fortunately, there are some general basic advances you can take to move from negative emotions and absence of discipline to a positive money mindset and extraordinary propensities.

We are going into the New Year and I'm certain that objective setting is at the highest point of your psyche.

Huge numbers of you are contemplating how you need to get in shape, work out 5 times each week, drink more water, clean up your home from start to finish…

Furthermore, presumably likewise on that rundown… getting your money together for the last time.

So on the off chance that you're intrigued, at that point continue perusing!

Money mindset is a basic, yet regularly ignored, part of accomplishing financial freedom.

We must have our psyche just before we can get our money right.

On the off chance that no one else has just disclosed to you this, I will: if your feelings are everywhere, you will never get rich.

To roll out certain improvements for the better, it is critical to search internally and looks at why your relationship with money is how it is. Discover how to change your money mindset to have a more certain relationship with money.

Peruse each one of those articles on propensities for the affluent, take seminars on making automated revenue streams, whatever. On the off chance that you accept where it counts you don't merit wealth, it won't come to you.

What you accept about money, yourself, and the world shapes how your life will unfurl. Every day you can settle on choices that will push you ahead financially or set you back. It's up to you.

You folks may have heard me talk about Ramsey money standards, similar to you should make a financial plan each month, live on short of what you make, and don't utilize obligation to pay for stuff. However, none of that is important if you don't trust it's conceivable to live that way, or in case you're not propelled to live that way. Countless individuals hit the nap button on their finances as though they'll simply awaken one day and have the option to resign. Perhaps they plan to pay attention to their money all the more sometime down the road. Or then again perhaps they think winning with money is just for "rich individuals."

The possibility that your money mindset is accountable for your financial life isn't new, even though it isn't yet all around acknowledged. A few people will excuse my affirmation that if you need to be financially secure, you'll need to manage your contemplations and convictions first.

However, in case you're baffled, worn out on being stressed over the future, burnt out on living without enough, and contemplating whether you'll have the option to resign, possibly you're prepared to have a go at something different.

You know that if you need to create new outcomes, you'll need to make new moves. In this way, whenever you've chosen, your mind will get mindful of chances you didn't see before—so focus.

That, yet you'll have to re-describe yourself according to the individuals who realize you by having new discussions with them. Consider these discussions your revelations; your stake in the ground, after having chosen.

Have you been pondering what you need to do to guarantee a comfortable retirement? Would you like to figure out how to invest now, so you'll have enough abundance developed to flourish in your brilliant years?

There's a major distinction between longing for getting rich and being focused on having financial freedom. Understanding this distinction is basic to collecting riches and setting yourself up for your future. To get this, you need to initially build up a solid money mindset.

It ought not to stun you to discover that every day perusing — a staggeringly straightforward errand — is a propensity normal to numerous independent moguls. 85% of moguls perusing, at any rate, two books for every month, contemplating different themes including authority, profession advancement, and everything money — including management and mindset. Here are ten money mindset books.

Routinely taking care of your psyche with information encourages you to push past restricting convictions (that in any case keep you down).

At the point when you train your brain to accept and get amped up for being rich, open doors will show up all over. You'll be more open to attempting new things, escape your comfort zone, and settle on what used to be hard choices.

I solidly accept when you ace your mindset, you'll ace your money. Here's a convenient dandy manual to assist you with the beginning.

Regardless of whether it's pursuing material comforts, financial autonomy, or the freedom that a "lot of money" can give, the human craving for wealth resembles none other.

In any case, the way to abundance is rough and loaded up with confusion.

Maybe the greatest confusion with regards to abundance is that lone individuals with a huge number of dollars in their ledgers are "well off."

Nothing could be further from reality.

Request that any three individuals characterize abundance and you'll get three distinct numbers.

On the off chance that you need to be well off, you'll need to think like the rich. Start by characterizing YOUR financial objectives: what amount of money would you like to have in a year? Five years?

Got a number? Great.

Presently on the off chance that you need to see a penny of that money, you'll need to build up an abundance mindset.

Chapter 1

What is a Mindset?

A mindset is a focal point through which you see the world. Like a couple of shades, it can marginally change what you see and how you consider everything.

Meaning of Money mindset can be portrayed as an assortment of emotions and considerations you have created over the long haul and still hold towards money.

These sentiments and musings will in general stem out of your very own insight of money or what you have seen around you.

Therefore a good money mindset will convey good sentiments and considerations towards money.

So at that point, it will be nothing unexpected what the impacts will be the point at which you have a negative money mindset.

Since it's negative contemplations and emotions that can direct disappointment with money.

For instance. On the off chance that you think having a lot of money is covetous, at that point you'll not become well off. For what reason would you if you believe it's insatiable?

Yet, what happens when you flip that over and accept that being rich is a gift? You'll begin to see the movement in your life.

You'll at that point comprehend that being rich isn't tied in with being avaricious. In reality, what you'll realize is that being well off permits you to be liberal. Abundance animates the economy. Also, affluent individuals are the top liberal suppliers to a good cause and other great aims.

There are a lot of other normal mindsets that limit your movement throughout everyday life. What's more, I show some of them further underneath. So continue perusing to perceive what they are – would you be able to relate?

Mindsets are contained convictions, recognitions, and mentalities that inform your considerations and choices.

Your money mindset is your general inclination towards your finances. It impacts how you settle on financial choices consistently and can decide whether you will accomplish your financial objectives.

Your money mindset is your exceptional allowance of faith-based expectations and your demeanor about money. It drives the choices you make about sparing, going through, and dealing with money.

Individuals who have a solid money mindset accept things like:

I have the freedom to spend, however, I can likewise reveal to myself no to a buy.

I appreciate helping other people who are battling by giving liberally.

I don't need to contrast myself with others.

It's conceivable to accomplish my financial objectives.

Your money mindset shapes how you feel about obligation, your mentality toward individuals who get pretty much cash-flow than you, how effectively you can give, your capacity to invest with certainty, and that's just the beginning.

Various mindsets are a significant piece of your toolbox for progress. Like glasses, they can darken your way or carry clearness to the street ahead. Developing a solid abundance mindset will assist you with adhering to your financial objectives and discover approaches to expand your procuring potential.

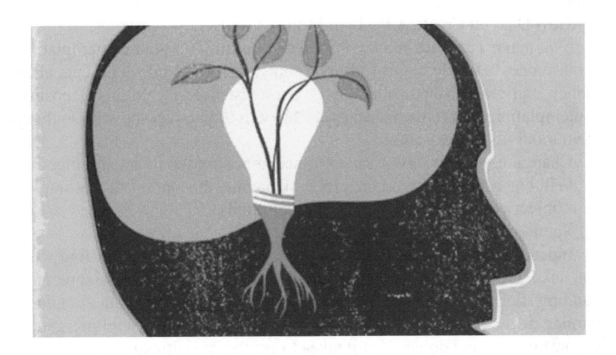

Chapter 2

What is an abundance mindset?

On the off chance that you dive further into the narratives of well off individuals, you'll notice an example:

Infrequently will a well off individual have the option to reduce their prosperity to a solitary marvelous second? All things considered, they'll refer to their mindset as the most compelling motivation for their flourishing.

An abundance mindset is an allowance of faith-based expectations, propensities, and practices that isolates the well off from the rest. An abundance mindset will control you to capitalize on the money you have.

In any case, it doesn't come simple. An abundance mindset implies spending less, making savvy investments, and searching for approaches to improve financial remaining with negligible danger.

Fortunately, with a little commitment, anybody can build up this mindset.

How Do You Create A Positive Money Mindset?

You make a positive money mindset by controlling your contemplations about money. Having control of your contemplations and sentiments about money can assist you in changing your existence. By intuition positive contemplations and remembering your objectives you can show these things in your day-to-day existence.

Changing your money mindset to accomplish your financial objectives

Without a doubt, the main piece of having the option to accomplish your objectives requires having the correct mindset.

Sounds basic enough right?

Indeed, it isn't generally that simple to hold your mindset in line while you take on the (now and again troublesome) long haul assignment of building riches. Achieving the correct mindset to assemble abundance implies dealing with how you think, chipping away at discipline, getting uncomfortable, and doing what it takes to get to your ultimate objective.

Improving your mindset is anything but a one and done sort of thing. Much the same as with the muscles in your body, you need to attempt to keep up it persistently else it will start to decay.

For what reason is the money mindset significant?

A money mindset is pivotal in deciding your activities and results. It additionally directs how you get and oversee the money.

If your money mindset is imperfect it can prompt obligation issues and overspending. Or then again it can prompt an undesirable craving to stick to your money. Also, because of the dread of being in need, you'll never permit it to be utilized for everyone's benefit.

This is never something to be thankful for.

Chapter 3

What is money?

Having the correct money mindset can be molded by understanding money itself.

I consider money to be an asset to get and do the things we need in this life. If you don't have it, by what method will you support your life?

Money is acceptable. Endeavoring to get more is acceptable as well. It's the abuse of money that is awful.

You abuse money when you:

Crowd it out of dread of need

Spend what you don't have (for example credit and advances)

Try not to bring in shrewd money moves, for example, sparing and investing.

Be that as it may, if you pair money with astuteness, trust me, you'll appreciate it quite a lot more.

Money changes lives. So if you're frightened to spend it, or spend a lot of then by what means will you are in a situation to transform you and the lives of others?

I never have enough or I'll never have enough money

This one I hear gracious too often. Particularly that word 'never'.

When you state you never have enough money, at that point learn to expect the unexpected. You'll never have enough money.

Saying this doesn't change your circumstance. Everything you're doing is reinforcing that you need more money. You're forestalling the critical thinking side of you to will work. This kind of mindset puts a conclusive finish to every one of your expectations.

Uncertainty forestalls movement.

How to change this money mindset?

Initially, it's alright to concur you need more money. Since it likely could be a reality that you don't. However, the key is to move away from what your circumstance says to what you need it to be.

You do this by asking yourself the accompanying inquiries:

What don't I have enough money for? Is it to purchase a home? To venture to the far corners of the planet?

What amount does (whatever it is) cost?

What amount do I have? (When you know this, you would then be able to ask…)

What amount do I need?

What would I be able to do to get this measure of money?

Do you see what's occurred here? You've transformed a negative articulation into a positive test. You've gone from settling to having an activity plan.

The initial not many inquiries recognize the need. The last inquiry gets you to plan something to address that issue. It's moving you to make a move.

At whatever point you end up going to state you can't afford something – stop. You can. The sky is the limit. It takes a touch of examination and understanding what's accessible to assist you with addressing this need or want.

Try not to remain in need. Bounty can and is for you.

I need more an ideal opportunity to bring in more cash

Who does have the opportunity? It's a bustling world out there and I get it. You got family, kids, perhaps an all-day work, companions to see, and occasions to go to. Where's an ideal opportunity to get more cash-flow, isn't that so?

Or then again is it right?

How to change this money mindset?

Let's face it. It's not about the absence of time but instead, it's an absence of inspiration and needs.

So right off the bat, build up a longing. Ask yourself:

Why is bringing in additional money significant?

For instance, is it to tidy up the Visa obligation approaching over you? For what reason is this significant? Is it to?

Be without obligation?

Quit stressing over money?

Be liberated from uneasiness?

At the point when you separate it like this, it makes want. You'll reconsider before you plunk down for hours before the TV.

Envision what it might feel want to be sans obligation. Doesn't this vibe better and increment your inspiration?

It's an ideal opportunity to get your needs altogether and appreciate the outcomes.

Rich get more extravagant, the poor get more unfortunate

In any case, what does that have to do with you? How can this affect your capacity to get abundance?

How to change this money mindset?

There is no uncertainty about a financial gap in the public arena today. Be that as it may, you would get further if you zeroed in on yourself first.

Try not to let society direct your financial future. Assume control over it.

Money is the base of all shrewd

This isn't valid for money itself.

We have been adapted to feel that way so that individuals who accept this won't accomplish more to get it. This isn't right.

Money is acceptable. It's the adoration for money that is underhanded. At the point when you love money so much that you'll do anything for it, that point, it's an issue.

View money as great. Since money changes lives. It transforms circumstances. It helps individuals.

When it gets into the correct hands, and afterward money does brilliant things.

I would prefer not to invest money into something if it comes up short

This one in my eyes is a key motivation behind why individuals don't step up in their finances.

There's an idiom: To bring in money, you need to go through money.

Understand that facing a challenge is something to be thankful for. Since nothing wandered isn't anything picked up?

On the off chance that you don't set aside the dread of losing and need you can't be available to get more than what you at present have.

The world's richest individuals invested in things and above all invested in themselves. The outcome? They get richer.

How to change this money mindset?

Right off the bat, quit stressing. Since everything stressing does is increment your dread of losing.

Also, understand more where came from. On the off chance that you can get money in any case, you can do it once more. So go out on a limb.

Change from dread of need to having confidence all things considered.

Conviction is central. It enables you to take a risk.

Money doesn't develop on trees

It's dismal because it makes a shortage of money mindset. You start to accept there's insufficient money. Or on the other hand, that money is hard to get hold of.

This mindset stops dreams. I mean why dream about a stunning home since there's insufficient money to get it.

You wait. Nothing changes.

How to change this money mindset?

To change from a world view limited by fear is to accept that there is sufficient money on the planet. Money goes around and there is all that anyone could need of it.

Money can't accept bliss

It can't. Bliss isn't something that can be bought. So once more, how can this affect you having money?

At the point when you think along these lines, it makes you accept that you shouldn't have things that will make life more charming. It resembles you've abandoned the option to have beneficial things.

Since even though money can't accepting joy, it can purchase food, drink, garments, and pay for cover.

Moreover, money can give some security. Envision how you would feel realizing you have a fat succulent annuity developing for retirement. Doesn't that fulfill you?

Money makes life simpler. What's terrible about that?

How to change this money mindset?

The vital thing here is to not cheapen money. Money is amazing and does a ton of good.

However, it's not intended to purchase joy so feeling this way is an exercise in futility.

Chapter 4

Speedy fire: Money mindset tips

Here's a gather together of how to change those negative mindsets into a positive one.

Distinguish the issue; at that point get over it by concocting a strategy

Know your reasons why bringing in money is significant. Since it reminds you when it gets intense – because it will get extreme.

Continuously have a dream and record it. Journaling and having a dream board is marvelous with regards to imagining what you need. This is so vital in achieving your objectives. You can get a diary-like this one.

State what you need to see – your words are ground-breaking. So in case you're stating or thinking any about the things over, it's an ideal opportunity to stop. Start and end your day with positive attestations.

Have confidence over dread. Eliminate uncertainty and dread because these are dream executioners!

Know there is a lot of money to go around and it won't run out.

Search for positive instances of progress with money and trust it can occur for you as well.

Practice Mindfulness

Another approach to dominate your money mindset is to rehearse care works out. Care gives the climate to hone your money mindset.

At times, the designs for your finances don't generally go-to design. How would you react to that?

Do you surrender and surrender?

A superior reaction is to recognize the circumstance, gain from what went poorly, and let it go.

Reacting in such a way is developed through care.

If you practice care, at that point you'll see a positive money mindset create.

Ways you can rehearse care

Mindsets changed what next?

To arrive at financial freedom, it's critical to add vision, objectives, and an arrangement to the blend.

Set your new money mindset to work. How are you going to push ahead? What plans will you set up to acquire more, spare, invest, and escape obligation? Record the moves you will make to get the outcomes you need.

Put them before you consistently so you see it. With the goal that you trust it will occur. Get a dream board and a diary to assist you with centering and work towards it consistently.

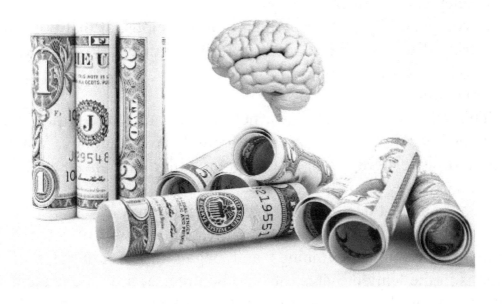

Chapter 5

Negative Money Mindset

You presumably have a poor or negative money mindset if when you consider money, it causes negative feelings, for example, dread, hopelessness, shortage, and overpower. It appears to be simpler to simply disregard your finances because the test appears to be outlandish.

Money doesn't develop on trees.

Presently, when you think that way, you consider money to be by and large scant and difficult to get.

Money is the foundation of all insidious.

If you generally partner money with malicious, at that point it turns out to be truly difficult to be excited about it. You begin to feel like it's a BAD thing to have a ton of money.

I'm simply bad with money.

This expects you can't learn new things and you simply acknowledge your destiny. You can't blame this for not having money. What you truly need to do is recognize that getting great with money is an exercise that can be scholarly after some time.

It takes a great deal of money to bring in money.

The biographies of the most extravagant individuals on the planet all came from humble beginnings and began little. A large portion of the tycoons in the United States (88% to be precise) are independent. Just 12% acquired a lot of money, and most didn't experience childhood in well-off areas.

You don't have to have a great deal of money to bring in money; you can start with a modest quantity and develop your abundance gradually. Consider it constructing a pinnacle step by step.

The rich get more extravagant, and the poor get less fortunate.

The issue with this is you're expecting your financial destiny has just been controlled by another person. Your financial future is altogether up to you.

I never have any additional money.

This is another reason for not having money. What you truly need to do is recognize that money management will permit you to have additional money.

If you have any of the restricted convictions I just referenced you will never be effective.

It's not your obligation or pay that is keeping you down. It's your mindset that you can't successfully change the circumstance that is keeping you down. This fair prompts you to abandon changing your financial circumstance and you don't do anything.

Chapter 6

Positive Money Mindset

If you have a positive money mindset, you will be bound to prevail during your financial excursion. With a good money mindset, you feel like no financial issue is difficult to survive.

You don't zero in on how awful your financial circumstance is; all things considered, you take a gander at what you can do to change your circumstance and spotlight on the way pushing ahead.

With a positive money mindset, you additionally take a gander at money from a position of wealth.

At the point when you take a gander at money from a position of wealth, you incline that you as of now have all that could be needed. If you as of now feel like you have all that anyone could need, you will relinquish all the unimportant spending.

You don't accept things to "cause you to feel better" since you're now content with what you have. You understand how honored you truly are, and perceive God has just furnished you with all you require to be glad.

So on the off chance that you have any of the restricted convictions I referenced before, I need you to think like this all things being equal:

There's sufficient money for every individual who will go out there and get it.

Money is an asset to do great in my life and for other people.

I will instruct myself about money so I can be acceptable with money.

I can bring in money regardless of whether I need to begin little

My financial future is altogether up to me and all I require to make abundance is as of now inside me.

I will deal with my money since when I do, more money comes my direction.

How Might I Change My Thinking About Money? (From A Negative Money Mindset To A Positive One)

On the off chance that you just spotlight what's going on with your financial circumstance, you won't be inspired to take care of business. All things considered, your spotlight should be on discovering answers for your financial issues.

You're not the primary individual to battle to cover their tabs or be this far owing debtor.

I've had a 6-figures worth of obligation from Visas and hospital expenses alone! Acknowledge that you didn't get yourself in this circumstance short-term, and it will likewise require some investment to escape this circumstance pushing ahead.

You can't move toward this financial excursion with a world view limited by fear or restricted convictions. At the point when you consider money, you should state to yourself "more where came from" rather than continually suspecting "I can't afford it."

Start by rolling out one little improvement. Make a financial plan and search for arrangements as opposed to zeroing in on the heap of money issues you have. Search for an exit plan as opposed to feeling stuck and sitting idle.

As I would see it, the initial step to tackling any money issue is making a financial plan or spending plan. A financial plan gives a great deal of information about your ways of managing money and permits you to see where you're turning out badly with your money.

If you need to utilize the equivalent planning strategy I use, you can look at my spending formats. These formats have helped me transform my 6-consider obligation along with 6-figure total assets.

My Monthly Budget Template

On the off chance that you think your circumstance is simply excessively overpowering and you need some assistance sorting out where to begin, pursue a FREE 15-minute financial appraisal and realize where you're financially solid and what zones could utilize somewhat more work.

On the off chance that you change your money mindset to be surer, you will search for circumstances as opposed to zeroing in on all the reasons you will fail.

Chapter 7

Begin Thinking about Your Money Future

Pushing ahead, I need you to begin pondering your capacity to procure, spare, invest, and escape obligation later on. Figure out what moves you will make to get the outcomes you need.

Yet, to do that, you need to comprehend your feelings of trepidation and weaknesses. Dread is a colossal issue for some individuals and can frustrate us from meeting our drawn-out objectives. Your financial feelings of trepidation right presently can be as:

A dread of disappointment;

The dread of being discovered by others;

The dread of weight and not have the option to accomplish your objective; or

Indeed, even the dread of squandering your money on another program just to discover it doesn't work for you.

So ask yourself:

What are my feelings of trepidation and weaknesses?

How could I arrive?

Shouldn't something be said about these feelings of trepidation that will keep me from pushing ahead?

For what reason do I think I need assistance?

Presently, that you have a superior comprehension of your apprehensions and frailties put forth a cognizant attempt to not zero in on your sensation of dread and spotlight on improving your money future. Your opinion and trust you can do, you will do.

The individual creation $1 million a year accepts she can make that much and will do that. It's everything she can see and her opinion about. She arranges the best way to do that, and she runs after that consistently.

So if you need to see changes in your money, you need to change your convictions about money.

Chapter 8

Instructions to Take Action and Make a Plan for Your Money

Since you've changed how you consider money, it's an ideal opportunity to make an arrangement for your money and how you will accomplish these objectives.

Ask yourself the accompanying inquiries:

For what reason would it be a good idea for me to begin this money venture or financial program?

What are my financial objectives?

What do I plan to achieve?

What is my WHY? What will persuade me to prop up when things get hard?

What is the 10-year, 5-year, 1-year objective?

When you have your financial objectives clear, begin making a move each day to assist you with drawing nearer to accomplishing those objectives.

Try not to Make This Mistake

The greatest misstep I need you to keep away from no matter what isn't investing in yourself. This is the BIGGEST slip-up I see tenderfoots make ALL THE TIME! They incline that they don't have the money, so they can't invest in themselves. Also, this is a BIG MISTAKE.

The greatest distinction between rich/effective individuals and individuals who battle financially is they're not hesitant to invest in themselves.

Rich individuals don't store their money and attempt to clutch each dollar—they utilize their money to get more cash-flow. They know by releasing their money that money will return to them with much more money.

I need you to think about all the manners in which you will invest in yourself pushing ahead.

At the point when I began my financial excursion, I got that on the off chance that I invested in the correct territories, it would all work out. On the off chance that I discovered somebody to direct me, I'll be signed in an ideal situation than attempting to sort it out all alone. On the off chance that I have the correct planning devices overseeing money would be significantly simpler.

I additionally realized that by investing in myself I would have skin in the game and will be not kidding about it.

So I need you to consider every one of those things. At the point when you perceive how much better your life will be, you'll understand you should've done this years prior! Alright, so will you begin investing in yourself this year?

How Is Your Money Mindset Formed?

Your money mindset is affected by various variables, including the brain research of money itself. The encounters you've by and by had around money will assume a major job. Things like on the off chance that you made some part-memories work in secondary school if you've been forced to bear liberality, or how straightforwardly your folks discussed money growing up.

Consider that last one for a second. Presently, all that occurs in your life isn't your folks' shortcoming. However, more is gotten than instructed, so how you saw your folks talk about money—or not a discussion about it—unquestionably impacted your mentality about money since the beginning.

Pondering how money was taken care of in the family unit you experienced childhood in will assist you with understanding the establishment of your convictions about money. In case you're hitched, this can likewise assist you with getting to the foundation of money battles you and your companion may have. Their experience was likely entirely unexpected than yours, which implies you folks are coming at this huge (and now and again enthusiastic) subject of money from two alternate points of view.

Chapter 9

What is a Poor Mindset?

The direct opposite of an abundance mindset is a helpless mindset. Most who have this "helpless mindset" don't understand they have it.

A helpless mindset is any of the accompanying: imagining that bringing in cash isn't right, that it very well may be managed without effort, that you'll never move out of the pit of obligation, or that you simply don't have the unique sauce it takes to build your income.

This mindset sabotages your money objectives and will effectively drive abundance away from you except if you work to neutralize it.

Choose to be financially effective

Getting to affluent begins route before you open that investment record or put aside that initial installment into your bank account. It begins with a straightforward choice, which in itself is an exceptionally significant one. It's concluding that you will be rich and that thus implies choosing to focus on the excursion and trust the cycle.

Concluding you will be well off (with full conviction) is an unfathomable lift to your mindset. This is because, with this choice, you are revealing to yourself you can do it. Except if you trust you can be rich, you most likely won't be slanted to take the necessary steps to construct abundance.

Decide your life esteems

Whenever you've concluded you will be rich, you need to decide your explanation behind needing this financial achievement. What's more, that implies deciding you're why. Your why drives a profound feeling of direction and encourages you to build up the inspiration you need.

Truth be told, having for what reason can straightforwardly improve factors in your day to day existence that tie into generally speaking joy.

So for what reason would you like to take care of your obligation, set aside cash, getting financially fruitful, financially free, and so on?

Understanding what you're for what reason will be your definitive spark particularly on the days or during the seasons when things are not going precisely as you arranged.

Relinquish principles and spotlight on the main thing to you

With regards to building riches and taking a shot at your money mindset you need to go with what works for you and its imperative to not become involved with guidelines that are characterized by the world. What's more, you likewise need to dodge correlation with others; it's the cheat of satisfaction.

Again this returns to your why.

You should resign youthfully; having $500,000 may be your meaning of financial freedom or maybe it's $1 million. Or then again your financial objective may very well be to have enough money to knapsack around the globe.

Whatever your objectives may be, center around your guidelines and what money intends for you according to what you need in your life.

Get comfortable with your apprehensions and your discomfort

Tension and dread are normal side-effects when you need to achieve something important. There's the dread of the obscure, the dread of progress, the dread of disappointment.

Also, on numerous occasions, dread can bring you to an abrupt halt and can turn out to be truly overpowering. Particularly when you fire making up things in your mind pretty much all the "what uncertainties" and "whatnots" around what could occur (that usually, never occurs).

The thing about dread however that is since it goes with the job you truly have two options. The best option is to let it keep you stuck. The second and better decision is to hold onto dread as a component of the excursion, let it join the party however let it know it's not permitted to keep you down.

One extraordinary approach to beat dread is to recall that you're "the reason" and glance back at all the achievements you've needed to date and the feelings of trepidation you defeated to arrive. If you could move beyond those feelings of trepidation you can most unquestionably move beyond your present apprehensions about money.

For each dread you have, there is presumably one activity (regardless of whether it's simply a little one) you can take to counter the dread. For instance, would you say you are apprehensive you'll never escape obligation? You can zero in on creating an obligation installment at this moment or sooner rather than later to neutralize that dread.

Chapter 10

Remind yourself continually

Regardless of how unnerving it tends to be, that you can do this and spotlight on making little strides each day before you know it, you will have gained huge ground.

Relinquish Past Money Mistakes

Whatever is keeping you down; you should sort out what it is and proceed onward from it.

Goodness my… I could compose for days about the money botches I made when I was youthful and even as of late. There are things in my past I wished I could return, eradicate, and do over; and rehash the entire cycle. Unfortunately, that isn't how life works.

When I acknowledged my financial disappointments from quite a while ago, I had the option to proceed onward from them. (Please re-read the last sentence.)

Beginning with a new point of view on money, for me, was a much-needed refresher.

It is the ideal opportunity for you to do something very similar! Relinquish your financial disappointments and begin to proceed onward. If you don't have the foggiest idea where to begin, experience our FREE course for Struggling to Financially Sound Money Boot camp.

Activity Steps:

Compose a rundown of your financial disappointments. Examine these with your mate, companion, or responsibility accomplice. Our FREE seminar on Struggling to Financially Sound Money Boot camp will go more inside and out on this.

What caused those financial disappointments? What did you gain from those financial disappointments?

Presently, you need to LET IT GO to push ahead!! Download this persuasive statement. Post it on your cooler, on your mirror, in the vehicle, changes your Facebook picture – wherever you can. Pinterest Fan – spare it to your sheets.

In conclusion, begin thinking ahead… What does your vision resemble?

Today is another day! The time has come to take a gander at your money from another point of view. Quit thinking about the past. Begin taking a gander at the new way you need to deal with your money.

Take out Scarcity Mindset

The viewpoint that everything is limited accepts there will never be sufficient.

In your psyche you assume, regardless of what you do that there will never be sufficient.

At the point when we were taking care of obligations, I had an inclination that I generally expected to purchase things for the best deal since I expected to squeeze each penny to get by. Nonetheless, I wound up spending more as a result of my viewpoint that everything is limited.

That sensation of there will never be sufficient.

With individual accounting records, a viewpoint that everything is limited can be inconvenient to your drawn-out progress with money.

In any case, by and large, that isn't accurate. There will consistently be sufficient; it may not be actually what we need or like. Yet, your necessities will be met.

Something contrary to a world view limited by fear is a wealth mindset. To have a solid relationship with money and move towards financial autonomy, at that point seeing your life and the things in your day to day existence through a plenitude mindset will be a distinct advantage.

Activity Steps:

Stop the examination trap with others. Be careful about the way of life creep.

Breaking point media utilization to short of one hour for the following week.

Put together and streamline your life.

Search for the positives covering up under the negative, troublesome circumstance close by.

These activity steps will assist you in defeating the world view limited by fear. Push past being poor and move towards a wealth mindset.

Reflect Gratitude

Be grateful for what you do have. Glance around and see what you have.

Show much appreciated!

A disposition of appreciation will consistently locate the positive and brilliant side of the coin.

This is something that sets aside some effort to rehearse. It isn't something that will occur incidentally.

Particularly in the predicament, reflecting appreciation is the hardest activity. I get it. I'm not wonderful at this one by the same token. In any case, you and I will be better by picking a demeanor of appreciation.

Activity Steps:

Compose at any rate 10 things you are appreciative of every day. Do this for in any event 7 days – far and away superior for 30 days

Open up your ledger. Be appreciative of every single penny. Try not to take a gander at the commas or the decimal's focuses. Zero in on every penny and show much obliged.

Consider the entirety of the beneficial things that have gotten to you where you are today.

It is the propensity an example of adding a penny reliably that makes an individual rich.

Recollect those pennies add up!

Set Money Goals

The initial three stages are approaches to transform the money mindset from negative to positive. Presently, the time has come to give that positive money mindset something to do. What are you going to achieve straightaway?

To have a laser-centered thought of what you need with money, defining money objectives are significant. Basic for long haul achievement.

It helps control your money mindset in achieving something – explicitly something that is line up with your greater life vision. You should know where you need to go in life to accomplish it.

Activity Steps:

Sort out your first money objective.

Choose the smaller than normal advances expected to take to arrive at your money objective.

Make changes to your money mindset to arrive at your money objective.

When you arrive at your money objective, returned it, and set another money objective.

For us, we chose to take care of our obligation in one year. We required an adjustment in our money mindset to get that going. That took commitment and steadiness, however, we were in the correct money mindset since it was something we needed to achieve to move to the following period of our lives.

Money objectives help your money mindset remain on target with what you need (and not society).

Related Reading: Avoid the Trap of Lifestyle Creep and Reach Financial Freedom

I Got This Attitude

This last one is something I state to my children every day at school drop-off – "you got this!"

In our adversely disapproved of society, it is a decent update that YOU GOT THIS. You can conquer this. This period of life won't rule your life forever.

This money mindset demeanor is only that a mentality. A conviction that the sky is the limit if you just put your money mindset to it.

You got this!

Activity Steps:

Put little updates in those spots where you need a jolt of energy token of "YOU GOT THIS"

Encircle yourself with individuals who trust in you and backing your choices.

Utilize your appreciation diary to help consider the entirety of the encouraging points in your day to day existence.

Simply recollect… you are commendable. You have a reason. Try not to let society pull you down. Remain above and alert. You got this!

Chapter 11

Offer thanks and attest yourself to progress

Offering thanks is a decent method to change what you center around. At the point when you are thankful, you center more around the things you have that you are energetic about just as on all the decency that has come to you.

Appreciation additionally drives happiness in your life which is vital to abundance building since when you are content with what you have, you are less constrained to spend, spend, spend, to increase material fulfillment which doesn't generally work since you'll see that there's continually something new that you can purchase.

Insistences are another truly astonishing approach to calibrate your mindset since assertions assist you with placing yourself in a perspective where you are regularly expressing what you accept to be valid and what you need to materialize which thusly keeps you zeroed in on the things you need and not the things you don't.

The Importance of Understanding Your Money Mindset

You do this in different territories without acknowledging it. Do you accept that causing your life partner to feel unique is essential to your marriage? Or then again that you need to have something important to pay lease? Or then again that "Pizza Fridays" are the greatest day of the week?

Your practices will uphold those convictions. That implies you'll most likely send writings to your companion for the day, appear at deal with time, and ensure you get pepperoni at the supermarket by Thursday.

Chapter 12

Money Mindset Tip

1: Let go of the past.

I realize that this is likely quite difficult.

In the past you have likely begun a spending plan… and afterward, quit.

Started sparing… and afterward spent the money spontaneously.

Perhaps charged a few things on your Visa that you lament.

We all have made a misstep with our money previously.

Be that as it may, we can't let those mix-ups characterize our fates.

Let the past be the past.

Try not to choose not to move on that you can't push ahead in the present.

Presently that doesn't imply that we shouldn't gain from our errors.

It's a good thought to reflect and gain from an earlier time.

I love beginning a money venture and thinking about exercises learned.

In any case, when that reflection is finished, leave the second thoughts before.

2: The circumstance will never be awesome.

Try not to sit tight for the ideal situation since they will NEVER come.

For instance, you may be trusting that your significant other will jump aboard with the finances so you can begin.

It's wonderful if your life partner is as amped up for this excursion as you are because two heads are superior to one.

Be that as it may, having your life partner on board is certifiably not a pre-imperative to the beginning.

It very well maybe 3 months or 3 years, before your mate gets on board with the spending temporary fad.

Meanwhile, start where you are, with the assets available to you.

Furthermore, continue supplicating that one day the person will get it. In any case, don't burn through significant time while the person sorts it out.

Something else that I regularly hear is that individuals are holding on to bring in more cash or improve paying position before improving their finances.

This is defective reasoning!

This line of reasoning expects that we will naturally be better with money once we have a greater amount of it.

What normally happens is that the absence of money management aptitudes turns out to be dramatically more terrible as we bring in more cash.

If we never set aside the effort to recognize our issues with money and change the practices (for example enthusiastic spending, motivation transportation, not esteeming the propensity for sparing), bringing in more cash will just exacerbate the money issues.

All things considered, focus on pushing ahead and improving your money now, regardless of whether you don't acquire a lot.

Since when that expansion comes, you'll be more ready to deal with it.

3: Be cautious with your words.

I regularly hear individuals participate in a great deal of negative self-talk with regards to money.

They make statements like…

I'm awful with money.

I'm awful with numbers.

I've never been acceptable with money.

I don't have the foggiest idea of how to the financial plan.

I'll never escape obligation.

Yet, on the off chance that you have that mindset, and you're continually those words over yourself, at that point you presumably will fall flat.

Words have power.

So pledge to just utilize positive words as it identifies with money.

Regardless of whether you've committed errors before, don't pound yourself. Rather reveal to yourself that today is another day. Furthermore, this time around, things will be extraordinary.

As you do as such, your relationship with money and your mentality and viewpoint towards it will improve all the while.

4: It's About Progress, Not Perfection

On the off chance that you set aside the effort to assemble your first spending plan, at that point that is progress!

It won't be amazing the first run through, and that is alright.

A spending class may be neglected, or a bill sum belittled.

You may even forget to accommodate your buys once or twice.

Be that as it may, it's alright.

Each great spending needs tweaking.

However long you are getting back up after you fall, that is the only thing that is in any way important.

On this excursion, we will all have difficulties intermittently.

So center on gaining ground, not accomplishing flawlessness.

5: Don't stand by until you are free and clear financially to begin carrying on with your life.

This is an exercise I needed to find out on my own.

Indeed, all of these tips have been significant in my own life.

Be that as it may, I feel exceptionally enthusiastic about this specific tip.

Kindly don't stand by until you're free and clear financially to start carrying on with your life.

There is an incentive in dominating the idea of deferred delight, especially on the off chance that you experience gotten into money difficulty on account of a YOLO (You Only Live Once mindset).

Yet, when we take deferred delight excessively far, we can coincidentally slip into a mindset of hardship.

If you cut out everything fun and eliminate all pleasure from your life to be sans obligation, you risk making yourself (and your family) hopeless all the while.

That degree of hardship isn't economical and stopping turns into the simpler choice.

Rather find a steady speed, appreciate life, and make room in your spending plan to live a bit.

For all intents and purposes, for me in my life, grasping this idea implied that my better half and I kept on going as we took care of obligation.

We went on almost twelve outings while we took care of 6 figures of the educational loan obligation and two-vehicle notes.

We settled on the choice to do so because we get a huge load of significant worth from having the option to travel and have new encounters.

Would we be able to have taken care of the obligation quicker if we had cut voyaging?

Indeed!

I might have shaved off a year or more.

However, travel wasn't something that we were happy to surrender.

So we decided to income trips while as yet making additional guideline installments to obligation.

Also, prepare to be blown away.

We took care of the obligation!

Understudy loans… gone.

Two vehicle notes… gone.

We got to the end goal and in the process, we have the entirety of the recollections and encounters that we had on those outings.

Presently, you may not be a movement addict like me, perhaps you make the most of your to-go espressos, those $5 smoothies, or your mani/pedis.

Whatever it will be, it's OK to hold a few things consecrated on the off chance that you get happiness and incentive from them.

Simply don't make yourself hopeless all the while.

Even though we are right now obligation free (other than the home loan) I need to consistently help myself to remember this and remind myself to appreciate the view en route to financial freedom.

Try not to be so centered on the location that I pass up the excellence of the excursion.

I'm watching out for later while making sure to appreciate today.

6: Move from a check to check attitude to an abundance gathering mindset.

Someplace on your excursion, this move ought to occur.

The second when you're done holding up fully expecting your check and no longer penny squeezing (even though those pennies do add up!)

Yet, you go from a shortage attitude to a wealth mindset.

I was naturally introduced to a lower pay family to two high school guardians who were simply attempting to sort out some way to be grown-ups.

As I progressed into adulthood and into my working years something that followed me was a shortage mindset.

It didn't make a difference how much money I acquired, I never felt like I had enough.

I was unwittingly reluctant to 'be without'.

So making the move to an abundance aggregation mindset has been hard for me.

On the off chance that you experienced childhood in a comparative setting, you also may battle with this.

What's more, provided that this is true, you may have to willingly volunteer to realize what abundance is, to figure out how to invest, and to contemplate the propensities for rich individuals.

Build up the abundance educational plan for yourself.

You may have to go to the library and get a few books, get a tutor, or mentor.

Get yourself a diary or possibly go to treatment!

Whatever it takes to work through the money issues and receive a bounty attitude.

In the remarks beneath let me know which of these money mindset tips you have battled within your own life!

Give Yourself Permission

No one is more inspired by your money than you. Not your companion, your companion, your financial organizer, or even your canine.

On the off chance that you need to change your money mindset, it needs to begin with you. No one else.

You may have no clue about how to expand your compensation, get more customers, or set more money aside for your retirement store. Yet, letting those reasons prevent you from pursuing your fantasies will waste your time.

On the off chance that you need to bring in more cash, you must be the one to request more.

On the off chance that you need to go on a multi-week get-away to Europe, you must be one to make those arrangements.

On the off chance that you need to start a new business for yourself, you must be the one that gets the clients so you can in the end leave your place of employment.

You're understanding this and thinking, I'm as of now doing the entirety of this. I'm making those terrifying strides.

Know whether you're still no place where you need to be, there are portions of your life where you're requesting authorization.

Take me for instance. A couple of years prior I was at an all-day work and working two jobs as an independent author. I was making enough to take care of the tabs to say the very least. However, I knew when it came time to end my work contract; I continued disclosing to myself I would search for another work. Consistently I would converse with my significant other about stopping and blowing up at all the costs we were paying for.

See what I'm doing here? I needed my significant other to disclose to me it was alright to leave my place of employment and work for myself. Some way or another, my significant other authorizing me made it alright to get independently employed.

All things being equal, he instructed me to do anything I desired. It was then I understood on the off chance that I needed to take the plunge, I must be the one to settle on the decision.

At the point when you request authorization from another person, you're restricting yourself. You're leaving your life (and money-making status) in another person's hands.

Allow yourself to acquire more.

Allow yourself to purchase those excellent shoes you've set something aside for.

Allow yourself to begin low maintenance canine strolling business.

Anything you desire.

So investigate your circumstance at present. What is it you need?

Activity Steps:

Start by journaling it hard and fast. Accomplish something as basic as working out assertions. As in "I need to bring in more cash" or "I need enough money to go on a get-away consistently."

A few people love to free compose. Locate a tranquil spot where you'll be undisturbed, sit still for a couple of moments, think about what you need and compose whatever strikes a chord for at any rate five minutes.

At the point when you record things, make no decisions. As in, don't let yourself know whether these things you need are correct or wrong. They're simply things you need.

When you have a rundown of things, reveal to yourself it's alright to have these things. Conceptualize how you will get it.

In case you're feeling yucky about the entire thing or you're not inclination the entire money mindset magic yet, utilize the accompanying layout and work it out. Recite it for all to hear. Does this process again until you feel this passionate longing to follow up on getting what you need?

Chapter 13

Manage Your Anxiety

It's a fantasy that fruitful individuals don't have something reasonable of impostor condition. Indeed, even the most extravagant individuals on the planet have negative money mindset musings every once in a while.

Money mindset authority doesn't mean you're feeling affection about your money constantly. You don't flee from your feelings, regardless of whether they feel net. At the point when you completely grasp what you're feeling, how you're feeling, and quit fleeing from it, that is the point at which the sorcery occurs.

At the point when you feel restless or let the feelings improve you, you won't settle on choices that advantage you. Envision for a second you're up for a performance survey at your particular employment or are pitching for new independent agreements. You're heading off to a discussion regarding why you merit a raise or potentially why you're an important colleague.

What are you thinking about this moment? Will you have the option to unmistakably explain everything you accomplish for the organization? Or on the other hand, will you minimize or convince yourself not to request a greater raise?

The way to a superior financial future is to eliminate passionate triggers around money so you can settle on choices from a goal outlook. Indeed, more difficult than one might expect.

Notwithstanding, there are numerous apparatuses to assist you in handling your sentiments and feelings around money issues. Attempt the activity underneath.

Activity Steps:

At whatever point considerations identified with money come up, grasp them.

Locate a calm place and record your contemplations. There are extraordinary journaling applications that assist you with recording how you're feeling and any situations that may have set off it.

When recording your considerations, compose what explicitly you accept to be valid about money. For instance, you're blowing a gasket about going out for drinks with your companions since you just have $20 in your financial balance. Where it counts, you trust you don't cause enough and to feel befuddled about the following stages. Record that!

After doing this take a full breath and reveal to yourself it's alright to feel along these lines. The purpose of this entire exercise is to rehearse not fleeing when things get awful. At the point when you figure out how to incline toward the discomfort, you'll be additionally ready to roll out the improvements important to improve your financial circumstance.

Since let's be honest, change is hard and will test your feelings.

Chapter 14

Forgive Yourself and Others

Forgiveness is quite a necessary piece of the money mindset dominance measure. It's tied in with clearing the psychological space so you can welcome better what might be on the horizon. Forgiving somebody or a circumstance is about you, not them.

If everything you're doing is holding sensations of disdain, outrage, and scorn, you're never going to completely permit yourself to make more abundance in your life. Additionally, when you're irate with an individual, a circumstance, or even the world, you're living with a casualty attitude.

Forgiveness isn't tied in with forgetting the occasions that occurred. It's tied in with relinquishing the negative or charged emotions so you can move onto more beneficial issues. Clutching disdain implies clutching the past. Making a superior financial future for yourself implies you need to look forward, and how to utilize your marvelousness to make it.

The hardest (and seemingly generally notable) individual to forgive is you. Consider each one of those choices you made, the words you stated, things you've done to hurt yourself as well as other people. Delivering those musings and decisions assists with welcoming novel contemplations, ones that can assist you with making real money.

At the point when my ex said a final farewell to me every one of those years back, I clutched so much annoyance and disgrace about the entire circumstance. I at long last forgave him and all the choices I made driving up the separation.

Inside seven days, I took care of the remainder of my charge card obligation. What's clever was that I had the money before, yet I wasn't happy to utilize it to take care of the obligation. Intriguing huh?

Notwithstanding, it's additionally insufficient to forgive and proceed onward. This should be an everyday practice. You will meet new individuals who cause you torment or others effectively in your life that has caused you a long period of torment. If there are things from your youth you haven't appropriately managed, do you truly think you'll let those go promptly?

Things to do:

Consider individuals or circumstances where you feel outraged or disdain towards (should be identified with money here and there). There might be a great deal and that is fine. No one will see this rundown aside from you.

Choose one that stands the most. Locate a peaceful spot, plunk down, and envision the individual or the circumstance. Permit any feelings to come up.

Either envision or state so anyone can hear, "I forgive you and decide to release these negative feelings." and feel yourself relinquishing them.

Do this process again.

Let lose Some Space

Stages 2 and 3 in a real sense assist you with clearing the mental mess. Presently it's an ideal opportunity to clear the actual mess.

It's not tied in with auctioning off things. It's really about clearing considerably more mental space when you dispose of actual things. Envision when your home is perfect and how distinctively you feel when it's a wreck. Same with having a monstrous heap of stuff you never use.

I wound up disposing of 90% of my things due to my craving for opening up space. Never did I envision it would lead me down the way it did. I figured out how to forgive myself for all my previous money botches and allowed me to be more and accomplish more.

I'm not saying you need to go insane as I did. In any event, getting out your wardrobe or curating your book assortment is adequate for now. Truly, your actual mess speaks to your psychological state. As in, would you say you fear relinquishing old convictions about money? Do you think that it's hard to clean up because you can't settle on a choice to spare your life?

At the point when you make space, you intellectually make space for new things as well. On the off chance that you need to get more cash-flow, you need to permit yourself to get the money. As in, give yourself the space to do as such by clearing convictions that aren't serving you. In particular, ones that keeps you from making much money.

A cool result is that you may discover lost money. I'm completely serious. There have been endless accounts of companions discovering money in boxes, coat coats, and books. I found a $100 greenback when I was wiping out my book assortment.

Things to do:

Begin cleaning up a room or things you infrequently use. Be heartless. Will you utilize these once more? If you use them once in a while, would you be able to get/lease them all things considered?

When you have a heap of things you need to dispose of, sort them by things to give, throw in the garbage, and sell. In case you're selling things, give yourself a timetable. As in, on the off chance that you don't sell things by a specific date, give them away.

On the off chance that you need to make it one stride further, offer gratitude, or offer thanks for the things you are giving up. They filled a need at one point as expected, and now you're delivering it to the world for others to profit.

On the off chance that you have a lot of things to clean up, start moderately. Tackle each room or classification in turn.

Chapter 15

Assume Liability for Your Choices

No one can transform you however you. It doesn't make a difference how crappy your circumstance is, how little you have in your ledger, or how little you think about money management, it's everything on you. The significant inquiry is, would you say you are prepared to do the money mindset work it takes to transform your life?

A great many people now will say yes however don't generally would not joke about this. They'll encircle themselves with motivational statements and imagine their fantasy life, however, don't do a damn thing about it.

Why? Since they're not prepared to venture up or accomplish the work it truly takes to be rich.

Venturing up methods assuming liability for your decisions, fortunate or unfortunate. Doing what should be done to excel. Deciding to move your point of view, whatever it takes.

The entirety of this stuff is startling. Trust me, I'm frightened most days. However, I realize that if I keep on assuming liability, quit seeing myself as a survivor of my conditions, there is no halting me.

At the point when you assume liability, you comprehend that the force is in your grasp. There is are countless occasions to be rich and do what you need.

So focus on changing your circumstance. You'll witness wizardry.

Activity Steps:

− Every time you want to whine, inquire as to whether it's something you can change. If not, let it go. On the off chance that you can, ask yourself how you can take care of the issue.

- Train your psyche to tackle issues. For instance, you need to resign in 5 years. Sort out an answer (or various) on the most proficient method to get this going. Even though it's smarter to begin little, express discovering replacements to fixings in a formula.

- If you can do this without judgment, locate a previous money botch or a circumstance you ended up in where you didn't deal with your money well. Conceptualize ways you might have dealt with it unexpectedly.

- Create another propensity where it expects you to propel yourself. A decent one will be one where it expects you to truly endeavor. For instance, I have a yoga practice and am running after doing handstands.

How Falling Into This Trap Will Limit Your Financial Progress – Awesome webcast scene from my companion Jen at Her Money Matters

Chapter 16

Be Grateful For the Flow of Money

You're most likely considering how you can be appreciative of money that hasn't come in yet.

To begin with, you will believe that the money will come. Second, you're appreciative of the inflow and surge of money.

Allow me to clarify. At the point when you're thankful for all the money you have, it welcomes more to come. That implies you're appreciative for covering the tabs. Thankful for getting a check. Thankful for a supper your companion purchased for you. You get the thought.

At the point when you're cheerful and feeling like you have all that anyone could need, that is the point at which you'll witness sorcery. You're available to more chances and imaginative answers for your money troubles.

Regardless of whether you don't become tied up with it, have a go at accomplishing something as basic as saying thank you when you cover the tabs. Envision the money is helping you keep the lights on, or give power to your oven so you can prepare dinners. At the point when you go shopping for food, consider the hundreds (truly, truly!) of individuals you're helping, from the ranchers to the individuals who convey produce, to the individuals who stock product at the store. Pretty wild, huh?

You need to move away from a position of need (otherwise known as a viewpoint that everything is limited) and step into a spot where the universe can convey the products. Everything begins with you trusting it can.

Things to do:

Start an appreciation diary.

On the off chance that you ponder, center around something you're thankful for.

Each time you get or part with something (like covering the tabs), state "thank you, more where came from."

Envision or conceptualize all ways you appreciate accepting or going through money.

Get Super Specific

How are you going to get what you need if you won't set aside the effort to sort it full scale? It's insufficient for you to state you need more money; you need to proclaim how a lot, from where and when. Or then again, do what I do, get very explicit on the sum you need and what it's really for.

This has to do with showing truly, yet it was more to do with your expectations. The vaguer you are tied in with something, the more outlandish you will let it all out. Being explicit likewise encourages you to envision whatever your heart wants. You can see it, believe it, and get amped up forgetting it. Therefore, it'll come to you much quicker.

Activity Steps:

Conceptualize your optimal way of life or something you're truly after. Sort out how much money it'll cost. Include somewhat more for no particular reason.

Implore, talk, think, or whatever it takes for you to begin a discussion with the universe about what you need.

Keep updated about the particular thing you need. Conceptualize approaches to get it

Imagine what you need each day. Get amped up for it. Accept you'll get it.

Chapter 17

Watch Your Words

You've presumably heard the expression whining is depleting. In addition to the fact that it zaps your energy, yet it destroys your money-making magic.

At the point when you're excessively bustling griping or pondering what you don't have or can't do, you're removing time from dealing with answers to acquire more. Additionally, in case you're continually revealing to yourself, you can't be rich, you'll trust it. Furthermore, you'll discover a wide range of approaches to discover proof of what you accept.

Begin seeing the inner exchange you have in your mind about money. Notice the words you use around others when you talk about money or accomplishing your objectives.

Here is a couple to look out for:

I should (Just because somebody is, doesn't mean you need to)

I have to (no one's forcing you to do anything)

I can't (generally?)

I wish (saying this causes you to feel like it's far off)

It's excessively hard (duh, work is hard)

Possibly (either accomplish something or don't)

Seeing and changing the words you use prepares your cerebrum to open up to arrangements and the conceivable outcomes to have more money. It'll help persuade and move you to make a reliable move; since that is the main assurance you'll have the option to get more cash-flow.

Things to do:

In case you're feeling audacious, challenge yourself to quit griping for seven days. Perceive how long you last.

If that sounds too overwhelming, simply notice the things you state around money. Diary it out or compose generally utilized expressions.

Change those normally utilized expressions into something more certain. For instance, if you disclose to yourself you can't afford something; ask yourself how you can afford it.

Here's a flawless little stunt on the off chance that you continually are negative: wear a versatile band on your wrists. Snap it each time you find yourself thinking or saying something negative regarding money.

Suggested Resources:

A Simple Experiment to Change Your View of Words–Amazing article by Joshua Becker of Becoming Minimalist

Experience Your Values

Your qualities are pivotal to you getting rich. At the point when you don't set aside the effort to evaluate and experience your qualities, you won't be upbeat. At the point when you feel hopeless, steamed, or like something's off, you'll wind up going through the money you lament.

The individuals who are or have been in buyer obligation are not experienced their qualities. Truth be told, the obligation is a genuine sign that something isn't right. As in, you're sitting around and energy on things that don't make a difference or add to your general joy.

At the point when you live in agreement with your qualities, you're all the more perceiving of how you invest time and energy. You'll see you go through less money and discover greater delight in your vocation. Or then again change vocations inside and out. You'll feel like your life has more reason which propels you to continue onward.

Your qualities assist you with developing and create personally. Or on the other hand, develop constantly a positive money mindset. It gives you an inward manual for a move towards all the abundance you can envision, to say the least.

Sorting out your qualities is simple. It's how you do them in reality that is hard.

Activity Steps:

Does a free compose practice about what you would go through if money were no article?

Gathering regular things and check whether you can sort out your qualities from that point.

Make a rundown and organize them from generally significant on

Whenever you have that rundown, make another rundown of things you'll quit burning through money on.

Make another rundown of things you need to burn through money on and make an objective to bring in enough cash to get it.

The Authentic Budget – Work on utilizing your qualities to make a money management framework that works

Chapter 18

Gathering It Up With High Net-Worth Folks

You're presumably worn out on hearing the expression about you being what could be compared to the individuals you spend time with the most. Individuals state it so regularly because it's actual. There's just so much inside work you can do, and in case you're encircled by horrible individuals, you will be hauled down with them.

If you need to be rich, stay nearby rich individuals. Or possibly individuals who have higher total assets than you do. If you can't discover them (or do not understand exactly how much money they mother loving have), look for individuals who a) straightforwardly talk about money and b) will discuss how they're pursuing abundance.

The web is your shellfish. Search our online forums. Start a book club. Take the necessary steps to locate those rich people, my companion.

One thing I've discovered to be excessively successful is to peruse individual accounting online journals. There are tons out there with ordinary individuals simply like you ready to share their objectives, battles and uplifting accounts of escaping obligation, resigning early, etc.

Online forums and get together gatherings are another incredible method to discover individuals. Bunches of urban communities have land investing get together. Regardless of whether you're not keen on investing inland, you'll in any event have the option to locate some high total assets individuals there.

Activity Steps:

Contact individual accounting bloggers and start a discussion.

Distance yourself from a portion of the truly antagonistic individuals in your day to day existence.

Keep Your Vision, Be Open to the How

At the point when you pursue getting more money, don't stress over how you will do it. Or then again don't stall out in one manner and not be available to different thoughts. The main thing to recall is to consistently keep to your vision. As in, what sort of life do you imagine? How would you like to feel? What kinds of encounters and things do you need?

Get clear on those, and let the universe accomplish the work to carry it to you.

Activity Steps:

Make the most of those changes.

Chapter 19

Transform Everything into a Game

Bringing in money doesn't need to be not kidding. You're improving your money mindset here, implying that the more sure vibes you have going your direction, the more everything will stream in support of yourself.

One approach to continue propelling you and assist you with pushing ahead is to transform it all into a game. Rather than all these genuine objectives, attempt and witness what might if you had a great time journey, rewards for up-leveling, and mystery codes to make gold tumble down from the sky.

Suppose you will likely acquire at any rate 6 figures this year. Is there an approach to remunerate yourself, a state on the off chance that you acquire $1,000 more than you did a month ago, what rewards did you procure? Would you be able to accomplice up with an accomplice or partner to see who can make more, similar to an agreeable rivalry?

I set an objective this year to compose a book on money management, just to check whether I could do it. I took the money I procured from the initial three months of deals and purchased something that brought me delight. I sufficiently made to take my child to the zoo, buy supplies for my nursery, and buy a couple of presents for my companions. I'm pursuing more pay from books.

Make Luxury Now

Making extravagance presently is about not exclusively being appreciative for all you have, yet accomplishing the way of life you need at this moment.

What's the purpose of this? It's to assist you with envisioning the conceivable outcomes. At the point when you find a way to make an extravagant or rich life, you'll begin to feel it's conceivable. At the point when that occurs, you get amped up for your objective. You'll begin discovering approaches to continue onward.

What's more, that my companions, is the purpose of dominating your money mindset. You need to psych yourself into accepting and feeling like you as of now have your most profound longings. It's everything close enough; it's simply dependent upon you to get it.

When you have that delineated (get as nitty-gritty as could be expected under the circumstances), allocate dollar adds up to them. What amount will it cost for each progression? At that point take stock of the money you have and what you can sensibly spend at this moment.

Go make the buy, feel how extraordinary it is that you have this wonderful thing/experience. Advise yourself that this is just the start of the astonishing things that will come.

Set Goals, Be Patient, Persevere

Not many wells of individuals got rich short-term. Building abundance is a moderate cycle.

Try not to nail your expectations of accomplishing abundance to unsafe "make easy money" adventures.

Set an objective for the amount you will spare every month. All the more critically—ensure that the arrangement you make for yourself is sensible and stick to it. The reason for a spending plan is to permit you to analyze your costs and search for territories where you can reduce or take out expenses. This cycle may expect you to settle on some troublesome decisions, such as changing to less expensive forms of items or staying away from extravagances through and through.

In case you're horrible at sparing and you expect to spare 10% of your next check, you have a higher possibility of fizzling and abandon your mission to get affluent.

Why not beginning at 1 percent?

Start little, support the propensity, and scale up after some time.

Chapter 20

Invest for the future today

A great many people imagine that money won't make itself... Or will it? The self-multiplying dividend is a cycle of development that permits your invested money to develop dramatically over the long run.

Accumulating funds happens when you procure interest on interest. Every year your money is invested, you'll acquire a level of revenue on the aggregate sum of money in the record, which incorporates the sum you made a year ago.

The more you permit your record to develop, the more money you will make consequently

Investing money is a crucial system among the well-off individuals—and you don't need to do only it. Figure out how to invest or search for help. There are a lot of refined and dependable counselors out there.

Letting the entirety of your reserve funds sit inactive in a ledger is a serious mix-up.

Pieces of candy used to be 5 pennies a pop. Today, you'd be unable to purchase Snickers for not exactly a dollar.

The supported expansion in costs over the long run for products and enterprises is called swelling. It diminishes the buying influence of money over the long haul.

If your investment system is to leave your money in a bank account for years on end, your savings will be worth very much less when you're at long last prepared to utilize it.

All things being equal, gauge your investment alternatives. Basic strategies for investing incorporate 401ks and Roth IRAs.

A 401k is a retirement plan that you can invest in yourself or through your manager. You may put money in it every month yourself or a little segment of your check is taken out each payroll interval and invested in the financial exchange. Businesses can coordinate your commitments, and your money will keep on developing until you choose to get to it in your brilliant years. Since commitments are made on a pre-charge premise — the money you put in can diminish your available pay for that year — you will pay an annual assessment on it when you haul the money out.

Another choice is a Roth IRA, financed by after-charge dollars. Thus, when you haul this money out, you don't need to settle any assessment, yet you can't lessen your available pay in the present.

An abundance mindset can assist you in searching out the best investments for your necessities. All things considered, who would not like to bring in money while they rest?

Chapter 21

Forgive Yourself for Your Financial Mistakes

There are likely a couple of individuals who can guarantee that they have NEVER missed a charge card or bill installment, never gone on an off the cuff over-spending meeting, and never attacked their reserve funds out of the blue. On the off chance that you are one of those individuals, you should most likely be the following financial master. For most of us, it's an ideal opportunity to rehearse self-forgiveness.

Comprehend Your Money Mindset

While you may think you know your demeanor towards money, it's conceivable that you're not completely mindful of how your perspectives are molding your dynamic.

Quit Comparing Yourself to Others

In this time of web-based media, unscripted television, and big-name magazines, it's excessively simple to get sucked into making examinations. We contrast ourselves with other relatives, to our companions, to superstars, and anecdotal characters on TV.

This is certainly not a decent method to invest your energy for a few reasons:

You're contrasting what you think about yourself (i.e., everything – "imperfections and everything!") to what you see of another person (i.e., their best side that they decide to show you).

Besides, you don't have the foggiest idea about the private subtleties of the other individual's finances. Somebody may seem to have an incredible life loaded up with impressive garments, get-away, and other fun stuff; however, it very well may be energized with MasterCard obligation... or more awful! On the off chance that you need a genuine model, look at the Real Housewives of New Jersey. Every one of that sparkles isn't gold.

At the point when you make correlations and end up lacking, you're redirecting consideration (and, possibly, movement) away from zeroing in on your finances and yearnings.

Along these lines, make feasible objectives for yourself and contrast yourself with those. Commend the successes and update your objectives as you contact them.

Make (and Maintain) Good Habits

When you have a few objectives and your eye on the prize, it's an ideal opportunity to set up the propensities that will guarantee you meet them. On the off chance that you've never dove profound into your pay and expenses or making a spending plan, this is a decent an ideal opportunity to attempt that. Understanding where you're going through your money will enable you to figure out where you can spare more if that is your objective. This mindfulness will likewise assist you with picking attainable objectives – regardless of whether they're a stretch – so you can expand on your prosperity as opposed to wind up incapacitated by rout.

One especially successful propensity is focusing on a set time – one hour out of each week – to survey your finances and screen your advancement. Overall, 8.4 hours out of every month dealing with their money. That works out to around two hours out of every week. You can utilize a platform like Mint.com, your ledger application, or a straightforward accounting page – simply make a point to audit everything.

In case you're seeing someone, a commonly gainful time for both of you and guarantee you will be completely present for the term of the discussion. In truth, money conversations aren't generally going great for couples, and contentions can follow. In any case, pushing through the discomfort can be the distinction between remaining together or separating for certain couples.

Enhance Your Budget for Happiness

The very word "financial plan" can fill individuals with fear since it infers limitations.

Practice Gratitude

The least complex practices can have a significant effect.

Hustle constantly

Since you have an establishment for developing your money, it's an ideal opportunity to invest in the main thing: Yourself.

If you need to encourage an abundance mindset, you'll need to limit time-squandering exercises like sitting in front of the TV or looking through online media. Around the world, we go through more than two hours via web-based media locales consistently.

Rather than burning through that time looking over, deal with your body. On the off chance that you're not previously zeroing in on your psychological and actual wellbeing, learn and practice "better wellbeing propensities, for example, eating healthy, resting right, and practicing the correct way.

Here another thought: practice your exchange abilities. Regardless of whether it's arranging your bills, your compensation, or a customer contract, well off individuals consistently beat the competition and can crush more dollars for themselves.

Make money as an afterthought by making side hustle. By driving for ride-sharing assistance, showing courses on the web, or in any event, administering weddings, 44 million Americans acquire a normal of $25 every hour with a side hustle.

Discover a specialty you're energetic about and it won't feel like work.

Learn new abilities in zones you're keen on as well. No one can tell when the expertise you adapted today will turn into an open door later down the line.

Chapter 22

Keep up an uplifting demeanor

Possibly you've known about the "law of fascination."

The law of fascination expresses that like pulls in like. At the end of the day, our musings and activities draw in comparative considerations and activities.

On the off chance that you think positive musings, positive things will occur.

If you consider making abundance, you will bring more abundance into your life.

You should cultivate positive considerations of riches and bounty. If you harp on the negative, you'll get debilitate and abandon your fantasies.

Start by eradicating negative considerations from your brain. Supplant them with contemplations like:

"I will be rich."

"I am adequate."

"I can succeed."

The way to abundance isn't simple; however, it won't be any simpler if you begin making potholes for yourself. You should be sold on the possibility of your prosperity.

What amount of time does it require to build up a Wealth Mindset?

The best piece of building up an abundance mindset is that you can begin quickly — by training, planning, and afterward activity.

The key is to begin little and tackle scaled-down objectives first. Like accruing funds, these little investments develop over the long run and further your advancement toward your abundance objectives.

Inside months, weeks, or even days, your abundance objectives will be on the road to success to progress.

Get It Going

There's no basic formula to follow for abundance. Perhaps you'll have a splendid thought and oversee it. Perhaps you'll begin a business with an extraordinary prime supporter. Possibly, as the vast majority of us, you'll buckle down—yet spare savvy and invest your way into wealth.

Toward the day's end, everybody needs to take the course that is ideal for them.

In any case, the individuals who make it to the end will be the people who can create and adhere to the abundance mindset.

Consider your life as of not long ago and ask yourself:

What did I hear and see about money growing up?

What's one thing my folks did with the money that I need to recreate?

What's one thing my folks did with the money that I need to do any other way?

Record your answers in a diary. What changes do you need to make? Part with some money.

Giving is the best time you can have with money. Furthermore, it's a demonstrated method to change your money mindset as well. It moves you on the range from narrow-minded to magnanimous. I realize you may feel uncertain from the outset, or possibly you're not paying attention to me. Simply attempt it! Focus on offering back some money to support an individual or association in need just once every week.

Chapter 23

Dream about your retirement.

Incidentally, in case you're as yet paying off debtors or don't have a secret stash, having a dream for your retirement is still unbelievably spurring. Take that fantasy and let it fuel your energy to arrive at a spot where you can invest significantly quicker!

Have the conviction that achievement is workable for you.

A few people have greater snags in their story than others, however, just accepting is the initial step. Your conduct will follow your convictions, making it simpler to adhere to great propensities. Also, after some time, your whole point of view will improve.

If you need to take in substantial income propensities stick, look at my fresh out of the plastic new book, Know Yourself, Know Your Money. We'll uncover and find precisely where your money mindset came from so you can figure out how to make an enduring change with your money. You can turn into the individual who trusts you can win—and once you accept you'll win, you will.

Chapter 24

Expert Your Money Mindset

On the off chance that your money circumstance isn't what you need it to be, you do have the ability to transform it. There are bunches of specialists who encourage that everything you contemplate money must be deconstructed, however, that is senseless, also overpowering. I've found and show a system that is unmistakably more straightforward and successful. Your center money conviction comes from your youth and is exceptionally shortsighted. You may even consider it a money fantasy.

For instance, somebody who accepts, "Money is muddled," would reliably take part in things like concealing money, being skeptical, keeping money at numerous establishments, maybe in any event, settling on arrangements that they don't keep, and lying about it.

We as a whole have channels for how we see the world, and an individual's activities on the planet are consistently an element of how the world happens for them (incidentally, this clarifies why a few people's activities appear to be so strange to you). The individual who accepts that money is muddled would have a channel that made those activities bode well.

They would accept that their activities were in response to money being muddled, never understanding that it's their actions that have money be confounded in their life.

Somebody who accepts, "I don't merit money," will probably have a day-to-day existence where they either don't bring in money or don't get a lot of cash-flows. Notwithstanding how brilliant, prepared, and significant they will be, they will reliably under-acquire their latent capacity.

At the point when money comes into their life, they'll part with it; deal with others first, maybe under the pretense of being liberal and supporting. On the off chance that they figure out how to spare a couple of dollars, they'll feel regretful about it, although setting aside cash is the best way to have an economical and predictable way of life.

In case you're continually dealing with others first, it may feel honorable to you in the present, yet the reality of the situation is you are setting yourself in a place to be a weight to others later.

To dominate your money programming, you need to initially remember it as programming. In Your Rich Retirement Academy, we ramble about frameworks. What are the frameworks and propensities you have set up in your life that reinforce your convictions about money?

In case you're prepared for financial transformation when you map out the money propensities you acquired from the past, you can make new frameworks intentionally that permit you to get more cash-flow.

One of my understudies who accepted that it wasn't alright to need money had consumed her time on earth living on low pay with bunches of charge card obligation. She was exhausted, however, and prepared for a change. Inside a couple of long stretches of finishing Your Rich Retirement Academy, she had taken care of her charge card obligation, yet had likewise begun a side business and was bringing in more cash!

She was radiating when she revealed to me that tolerating that initially paying customer felt like a tremendous victory over the past.

Chapter 25

Overcome Your Fears

Dread is a feeling individuals advanced into having. It secured us and helped the species endure. It had us move immediately when looked at by a saber-toothed tiger, so it filled a significant need. Presently, nonetheless, most apprehensions are developmental remainders that serve just to restrict and trap us. For the brain, whatever isn't as of now something we realize we can endure causes dread.

We regularly feel dread when confronted with a circumstance that will extend or expand our latent capacity. Open doors for development cause dread—and on the off chance that you decide to follow up on the dread and remain in your comfort zone, you'll never get more cash-flow. One thing to note about dread: If you're encountering dread, what you are doing is envisioning something occurring later on. It's tied in with something that isn't going on at this point.

In that sense, dread is unreasonable, and its capacities to keep you out of doing great arranging and making moves to evade terrible results.

You may be anxious about the possibility that you won't have the option to resign with enough, or apprehensive that you can't support your youngster's schooling, and that dread may feel genuine, yet notice that it's not happening now.

On the off chance that you need to begin getting more cash and have financial security, you need to control your dread. Being halted by dread will keep you broke and cause you to feel broken?

Conclude that You Are Going to Make More Money

What about that? Simply choose.

"On the off chance that it is to be, it is up to me!"

All things considered, you're just a single answerable for your financial achievement.

Nobody else.

Not your accomplice, your mate, your dad, your companions, or your chief.

To choose in a real sense intends to slaughter off the entirety of different other options—so in case you're truly prepared to get more cash-flow, you must initially choose and get 100% submitted.

At this moment, today, if you need more than you have, the initial step is to conclude that you will get more cash-flow.

Your aims have power!

(Have you chosen at this point? Proceed. At present. It's FREE.)

Make New Moves, Fail Fast, and Improve to Build the Skill of Making More Money

Whenever you've concluded that you will get more cash-flow, the wizardry of the universe is that open doors will introduce themselves for you to do exactly that, yet you'll need to remember them. My money programming reveals to me that there will never be sufficient money, so obviously I'm slanted to botch chances to procure it. I frequently think, "That will never work for me," or, "I'm not qualified." I've discovered that those musings are regularly pointers that I'm being given a substantial method to bring in money! You know that if you need to deliver new outcomes, you'll need to make new moves. Thus, whenever you've chosen, your cerebrum will get mindful of chances you didn't see before—so focus. That, however, you'll have to re-portray yourself according to the individuals who realize you by having new discussions with them. Consider these discussions your affirmations; your stake in the ground, in the wake of having chosen.

On the off chance that you can't consider what to say, here are a few plans to kick you off:

"I'm hoping to raise my family unit incomes—have you ever done that? Do you have any thoughts for me?"

"I will get more cash-flow this year than I did a year ago, so I'm attempting to sort out how I will do that. Do you know somebody I should converse with?"

"Have you ever begun a side business or acquired side pay? I will get familiar with some great approaches to do that for myself. Do you have any recommendations?"

Notice none of these sentences have, "need" in them. You're GOING to do it, not have to do it. Bunches of individuals need more money to live well—you're GOING to get more cash-flow since you said as much and you're the one in particular who can make it valid.

One significant new move I prescribe you make is to mechanize your finances.

Mechanizing permits you to increase all-out lucidity about precisely the amount more money you need to make, the amount you can spend to remain on the arrangement, and assists with setting up frameworks that ensure the aggregation of money accurately for what you esteem most.

I mentor individuals through the whole cycle of robotizing their finances in my accounting and life transformation course, Your Rich Retirement Academy. I've been utilizing mechanization in my very own finances for years and prescribe it to everybody!

A portion of my understudies have utilized computerization to take care of a huge number of dollars of obligation, and others have utilized it to twofold and significantly increase their reserve funds. Mechanization has the special reward of permitting you to aggregate assets for what you most need to go through money to do. Robotizing truly works.

Become somebody who says yes to things, and test approaches to get more cash-flow. It's an expertise, and you construct it over the long run.

It's an ideal opportunity to invest in you.

If you have confidence in yourself, consider yourself to be a financially autonomous individual, and work on being whom you need to become . . . it will in the end occur!

Pause for a minute to imagine your future self. I consider this activity the "Recliner Technique."

Close your eyes and undertaking yourself forward to when you're 80 years of age.

See yourself discussing with your more established, savvier self.

Request that your future self-offers you clear and exact responses to the accompanying inquiries: What would it be advisable for me to quit doing? What would it be advisable for me to begin doing? Is there anything you'd change about your life?

Tune in for the appropriate responses; permit the information to saturate your mind . . .

At the point when you're prepared, open your eyes, and record what your future self said to you.

You need to encounter your optimal way of life, isn't that so? So by what means will you notice the counsel you got from your future self? In what manner will you bring in enough money so you can understand your objectives and dreams? Furthermore, when you're financially free, by what means will you get your psyche prepared to deal with your money? By what method will you invest your money admirably? These are immeasurably significant inquiries to pose.

Comprehend what money is . . . Also, your relationship with it.

Money is a thought that was made to set up a worth framework. It's a method for reasonable trade between those associated with exchanges, for example, exchanging and investing. So money is just a thought. Also, thoughts are just electromagnetic energy.

Nonetheless, factors other than pondering money add to its stream and dissemination into and out of your hands and financial balance. When you comprehend the neuroscience behind pulling in and acquiring as much as you need, things will turn into a great deal more clear and simpler.

Chapter 26

Worth yourself above all else.

There's an adage: "We don't consider them to be for what it's worth. We just consider them to be as we may be." The money results you're encountering are an impression of your inside structure. At the point when you change your psychological outline and financial mental self-portrait you transform outside outcomes.

If you continue revealing to yourself that you're not shrewd enough or adequate, or that you don't know enough, it won't be anything but difficult to turn on the constant flow of income. Furthermore, with a fixed, low-acquiring mindset and steady negative self-talk, you won't probably resign early.

So rather than such ineffective reasoning, execute a "tycoon mindset" and put a high incentive on you. At the point when you esteem yourself most importantly, you increment your meriting level through a self-esteem vibration and reverberation.

Adjust your feelings to your objectives.

If you don't have an enthusiastic motivation behind why you need to achieve your financial objectives and dreams, you won't have the important fuel to keep you spurred when self-uncertainty and dread appear to smash them.

You should utilize your feeling and your higher reason as fuel. Would you like to have enough money to help spare the ocean turtles? Would you like to have the option to invest more energy with your friends and family? Would you like to mend yourself and help other people to recuperate themselves? In what manner will your financial achievement make a day to day existence brimming with reason and significance for you and your qualities?

You can't simply set objectives. You need to get each cell of your general existence engaged with your objective cycle. This is the mystery fixing to finishing your objectives to culmination.

Recollect the discussion you had with your more seasoned, smarter self? Fuse that insight into your objective setting and arranging. Make a rundown of your explanations behind defining objectives. For what reason would you like to accomplish your fantasies?

Sort out what spurs you.

At the point when you set huge objectives, you need to switch your reasoning, convictions, and practices. Also, this reworking takes a ton of training and commitment. As people, our minds are wired to a dread circuit . . . furthermore, thus, we love our comfort zone. We dread the obscure, so we remain smug and lenient toward our current (not ideal) circumstances.

So my next inquiry to you is about inspiration. Do you have a large enough rationale for making a move on your objective/dream?

Presently ask yourself: Does it matter to me if my life has genuine reason or importance? The explanation I need you to pose yourself this inquiry is that the appropriate response may assist you with superseding your present natural and mental wiring that keeps you stuck in the comfort zone.

Help your abilities and make an arrangement.

When you're clear about what you need and why you need it, the following stage is to increase further knowledge on the most proficient method to achieve your objectives and dreams. You need to sort out what truly propels you to be focused on making a move toward your objectives.

How about we accept the money as an energy idea above and beyond and add this assertion: You will get paid in the direct extent to the administration and worth you bring to the commercial center for which you charge.

On the off chance that you are presently not acquiring all that anyone could need, this is because you are not yet offering enough of your administrations, information, and aptitude to either enough individuals or the correct individuals. Keep in mind, money is important for a worth framework, and the more you get individuals to esteem what you offer, the more you will acquire . . .

Ask yourself these inquiries:

What must I realize?

What abilities must I overhaul?

What convictions and propensities must I create?

What convictions and propensities must I let go?

Who can assist me with accomplishing this?

When you have the appropriate responses and are clear about what you should do, make an arrangement, and begin making a prompt move. You've likely heard that an objective or a dream without an arrangement is just a fantasy. Be that as it may, with an arrangement, you can make your fantasy your existence. Nobody unearths accomplishment without a vital arrangement. Get away from where you need to go, whom you need to be, and what you need to achieve.

It is safe to say that you are prepared to build up a solid, rich, money mindset?

Money is anything but difficult to acquire if you do a couple of things right, and it will forever escape you if you disregard these fundamental standards. The equivalent is valid about overseeing, investing, and setting aside cash. To have more pay, you should have the correct mindset. Furthermore, when you have that, you can find a way to bring in your money effortlessly develops for you and your optimal future . . .

Chapter 27

Conclusion

Notwithstanding your money mindset at present, you can change your money convictions to be something other than what's expected and more certain. At the point when you change your money mindset, that is the point at which you can genuinely begin your financial excursion and plan your fantasy financial life.

Get the financial apparatuses you need or exhortation from somebody who has been the place where you are and has demonstrated they realize how to accomplish the objectives you plan to accomplish.

Having the correct money mindset can have a significant effect on accomplishing your life and financial objectives. It will be that as it may, require consistent concentration and sustaining.

It's tied in with setting the correct expectations and keeping your objectives top of the brain. You are more than fit for changing and improving your money mindset and the prizes will be well justified, despite all the trouble.

Note: This e-book is optimized for viewing on a laptop screen, however it is prepared so you can also print it out and gather it as a book. Since the textual content is optimized for display screen viewing, the kind is large than that in traditional printed books

CPSIA information can be obtained
at www.ICGtesting.com
Printed in the USA
LVHW061056180521
687737LV00004B/262